GEMS
NATURE'S JEWELS
TOPAZ

By Caitie McAneney

Gareth Stevens
PUBLISHING

Please visit our website, www.garethstevens.com. For a free color catalog of all our high-quality books, call toll free 1-800-542-2595 or fax 1-877-542-2596.

Library of Congress Cataloging-in-Publication Data

McAneney, Caitlin, author.
 Topaz / Caitie McAneney.
    pages cm. — (Gems : nature's jewels)
 Includes bibliographical references and index.
ISBN 978-1-4824-2872-8 (pbk.)
ISBN 978-1-4824-2873-5 (6 pack)
ISBN 978-1-4824-2874-2 (library binding)
1. Topaz—Juvenile literature. 2. Precious stones—Juvenile literature. I. Title.
 QE391.T6M33 2016
 549.62—dc23

                                    2014048077

First Edition

Published in 2016 by
Gareth Stevens Publishing
111 East 14th Street, Suite 349
New York, NY 10003

Copyright © 2016 Gareth Stevens Publishing

Designer: Andrea Davison-Bartolotta
Editor: Kristen Rajczak

Photo credits: Cover, p. 1 © iStockphoto.com/SunChan; p. 4 Albert Russ/Shutterstock.com; p. 5 (main) J. Palys/Shutterstock.com; p. 5 (inset) Nastya22/Shutterstock.com; p. 6 www.sandatlas.org/Shutterstock.com; p. 7 Azuzi/Shutterstock.com; pp. 8–9 (mountains) Tweeber69/Wikimedia Commons; p. 9 (topaz) Biophoto Associates/Getty Images; p. 11 DEA/A. Dagli Orti/Getty Images; p. 13 Joel Arem/Getty Images; p. 15 (inset) courtesy of the Metropolian Museum of Art; p. 15 (main) Manederequesens/Wikimedia Commons; p. 16 Nantpipat Vutthisak/Shutterstock.com; p. 17 (inset) Byjeng/Shutterstock.com; p. 17 (main) Imfoto/Shutterstock.com; p. 18 T photography/Shutterstock.com; p. 19 N Mrtgh/Shutterstock.com; p. 20 Observer31/Wikimedia Commons; p. 21 Mahesh Patil/Shutterstock.com.

Printed in the United States of America

CPSIA compliance information: Batch #CS15GS: For further information contact Gareth Stevens, New York, New York at 1-800-542-2595.

Contents

What Is Topaz?. 4

Becoming Topaz 6

Finding Topaz 8

The Look and Feel of Topaz. 10

Topaz on Fire! 12

History and Legends 14

Topaz Jewelry 16

The Value of Topaz 18

Rare Topaz. 20

Glossary. 22

For More Information. 23

Index 24

Words in the glossary appear in **bold** type the first time they are used in the text.

What Is Topaz?

Topaz is a **gem** of many colors! It's a **mineral** that forms crystals. These crystals can be yellow, brown, red, or colorless. Sometimes the crystals are even purple, blue, or pink. Some topaz colors happen naturally. Other times, the stone is treated in a lab to make a color, such as deep blue.

The name "topaz" may have come from the Sanskrit word "tapas," which means "fire." That might be because topaz is best known for being a beautiful golden color.

The beauty of topaz makes it a very popular gem.

Becoming Topaz

The most important thing that's needed to make topaz is heat! Topaz is commonly found in mountains that once were active **volcanoes**. These mountains are made of a lot of igneous rock. Igneous rock starts as liquid rock, or magma, deep within Earth.

When the magma cools to form igneous rock, crystals may start to form. A certain gas is given off as this happens, containing the **element** fluorine. Fluorine causes the crystals to become topaz.

rhyolite ▶

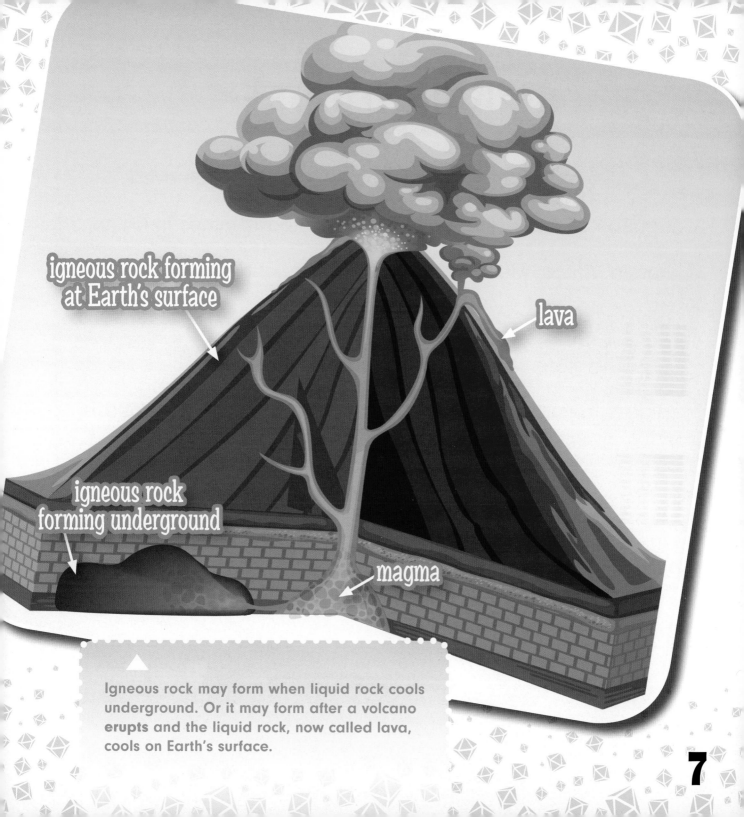

igneous rock forming
at Earth's surface

lava

igneous rock
forming underground

magma

Igneous rock may form when liquid rock cools underground. Or it may form after a volcano erupts and the liquid rock, now called lava, cools on Earth's surface.

7

Finding Topaz

Like many other gems, topaz is mined, or removed from other rock using tools. There are topaz mines in China, Russia, Africa, Mexico, Australia, Japan, and many other places.

The state of Minas Gerais in Brazil is one of the best places to find topaz. Two mines in Ouro Preto, Minas Gerais, are the only places where a special yellow-orange topaz called imperial topaz can be found. Unfortunately, so much imperial topaz has been mined there soon may not be any left.

Topaz Mountain

Sometimes, topaz can be found in metamorphic rocks, or rocks that have been changed over time because of high heat or pressure.

▲

Topaz is the state gem of Utah. It's found in Utah's Topaz Mountain. People find golden-colored topaz there that turns colorless when in sunlight for a long time.

The Look and Feel of Topaz

Topaz often has large crystals. The crystals' colors **vary** by the location in which they're found. Topaz's luster, or ability to **reflect** light, is vitreous, meaning that it's like glass. In addition, no matter what color the gem is, topaz is transparent. That means you can see through it!

Topaz is one of the hardest gems. However, it can break apart if it's not handled with care. When a gem splits easily, it's said to "cleave" easily.

Be a Gem Genius!

Mineral hardness is measured on the Mohs scale. This scale measures hardness by a mineral's ability to scratch a softer mineral. Topaz is an 8 out of 10 on the Mohs scale, which means it's very hard.

In the 1800s, pink topaz was found in Russia. The czar, or Russian ruler, let only his close family and friends wear pink topaz as a sign of royalty.

Topaz on Fire!

Sometimes, miners find colorless or light-colored topaz. This topaz might be made into different colors through irradiation and heat treatment.

Irradiation is when a gem is exposed to radiation, or certain waves of energy. Irradiation changes the crystal **structure** of the gem, which makes it look different in the light. For example, lab workers use irradiation to turn light-blue topaz into brown topaz. Then, they heat it to a high temperature, which changes the stones to a dark blue.

Be a Gem Genius!

Some radiation isn't safe for people. Because of that, there are rules about selling blue topaz. It needs to be stored for a while before selling so the irradiated matter is no longer harmful.

Because of irradiation and heat treatment, more colors of topaz are available than ever before!

History and Legends

People have used topaz for thousands of years. In ancient times, topaz was sometimes made into powder to treat sickness! Many **civilizations** had their own **legends** about topaz. Some believed it had special powers.

The ancient Egyptians believed yellow-orange topaz was from the sun god, Ra, and could keep the wearer safe. The ancient Romans also connected topaz to the king of their gods, Jupiter. The ancient Greeks thought topaz gave strength to the person who wore it.

Be a Gem Genius!

Some people believed topaz would change color if near food or drinks that were poisoned!

The ancient Greeks believed topaz could make the owner invisible if they were in harm's way.

Roman topaz ring stone

Topaz Jewelry

Topaz is a very popular gem that's used to make **jewelry**. That's because it's pretty easy to find and can be treated to turn many colors. People who make topaz jewelry use special lapidary, or gem-cutting, tools. They shape the gem by creating many facets, or small, flat surfaces. Then, they mount the gem in a setting, such as a necklace or ring.

Golden topaz is the birthstone for the month of November. People born in November may receive topaz jewelry!

blue topaz necklace
▼

Be a Gem Genius!

When a jewel has many facets, it catches the light and really sparkles!

facet

Topaz jewelry can be mistaken for other kinds of jewelry. Clear topaz, also called mystic topaz, has been mistaken for diamonds.

The Value of Topaz

Topaz's value is often based on the commonness of its color. The less common the color, the more **valuable** the gem is. One of the most valuable kinds of topaz is imperial topaz. That's because there's a limited amount of it in the world. Red and orange topaz increase in value the deeper their color is, too.

A topaz's value also depends on a gem's mass. A carat is a unit of measurement for the mass of gemstones. The more carats a gem has, the more valuable it is.

imperial topaz

The best British topaz is found in the Cairngorm Mountains in Scotland.

Rare Topaz

The El Dorado Topaz is 31,000 carats and is the largest faceted gemstone in the world! The Lua de Maraba Topaz is the world's second-largest faceted topaz at 25,250 carats. One famous topaz in history was called the Braganza Diamond. Belonging to Portuguese royalty, this colorless topaz was mistaken for a huge diamond!

The American Golden Topaz is the largest cut yellow topaz. It's on display at the Smithsonian National Museum of Natural History in Washington, DC.

American Golden Topaz
22,892.5 carats
Minas Gerais, Brazil

As you move around this remarkable gem, watch how light flashes off its 172 facets. At 4.6 kg (10.1 lb), it is one of the world's largest gems. Gem-cutter Leon Agee fashioned it over the course of two years in the late 1980s from an 11.8-kg (26-lb) crystal.

Gift of the Rockhound Hobbyists of America through the efforts of the six regional federations of mineralogical societies and Drs. Marie and Ed Borgatta, 1988   G9875

Finding Famous Topaz in the US

Chalmers Topaz
5,899.5 carats
Field Museum of Natural History

Brazilian Princess Topaz
21,005 carats
American Museum of Natural History

Lindsay Uncut Topaz
70 pounds (32 kg)
Smithsonian National Museum of Natural History

Gold Topaz Sphere
12,555 carats
Smithsonian National Museum of Natural History

Freeman Uncut Topaz
111 pounds (50 kg)
Smithsonian National Museum of Natural History

Glossary

civilization: organized society with written records and laws

element: matter, such as fluorine, that is pure and has no other type of matter in it

erupt: to burst forth

gem: a stone of some value that is cut and shaped

jewelry: pieces of metal, often holding gems, worn on the body

legend: a story that has been passed down for many, many years that's unlikely to be true

mineral: matter in the ground that forms rocks

reflect: to give back light

structure: the way something is arranged

valuable: worth money

vary: to be different or to become different

volcano: an opening in a planet's surface through which hot, liquid rock sometimes flows

For More Information

Books

Squire, Ann O. *Gemstones.* New York, NY: Children's Press, 2013.

Tomecek, Steve. *Everything Rocks and Minerals.* Washington, DC: National Geographic, 2010.

Websites

Earth Facts: Rocks and Minerals
www.sciencekids.co.nz/sciencefacts/earth/rocksandminerals.html
Read about rocks and minerals, including the different kinds and how they're made and identified.

Minerals, Crystals, and Gems
www.smithsonianeducation.org/educators/lesson_plans/minerals/gems.html
Explore this Smithsonian Education lesson about what minerals, crystals, and gems are and how they're formed.

Index

American Golden Topaz 20

birthstone 16

Braganza Diamond 20

Brazil 8

Brazilian Princess Topaz 21

Brazilian ruby 19

carats 18

Chalmers Topaz 21

colors 4, 10, 12, 13, 16, 18

Egyptians 14

El Dorado Topaz 20

facets 16

fluorine 6

Freeman Uncut Topaz 21

Gold Topaz Sphere 21

Greeks 14, 15

hardness 10

heat treatment 12, 13

igneous rock 6, 7

imperial topaz 8, 18

irradiation 12, 13

jewelry 16, 17

legends 14

Lindsay Uncut Topaz 21

Lua de Maraba Topaz 20

luster 10

metamorphic rocks 9

Minas Gerais 8

mines 8

Mohs scale 10

mystic topaz 17

pink topaz 11

Romans 14

Russia 11

Utah 9